Richard Meier Collages

Gagosian Gallery

Richard's Almanac: Scissors Pleasure Plane Paper
By David Shapiro

The theory of collage is itself by now a collage. In a brilliant avowal Meyer Schapiro links Picasso's and Braque's cubist collages, their *jouissance*, as an old story of medieval uses of differing textures of oil and gold. In a literalist mode, Jasper Johns once told me he used bits of newspaper, because "the whole idea of a newspaper is to turn it over, isn't it?" Dada collage attacks and desecrates. The meeting of the sewing machine and umbrella on the surgical floor, I mean table, has grown from Lautréamont's formula to Breton's convulsive and mad love. What Samuel Johnson deplored as the violent yoking of disparate images in the metaphysical poets has become the fundamental conceit, as in the houses of Cornell, where Fairfield Porter found the "highest and lowest reaches" of the human spirit. High and low, those fabulous chimeras, surge toward the options of desecration, *détournement*, and demobilization. Now their practice of collage is an historical form as dense with changes as assemblage, *objet trouvé*, and lost objects. But the architect—what has he to do with this gluing, cutting, and the trickster's scissors, this sticky art without rocks, but not without the scholar's paper and planarity?

The architect and the collage are another old system, from Colin Rowe to Eisenman, who told me he preferred the word "graft" to "collage," where his discontinuities prevailed. The significant issue for John Hejduk was the hand's auratic storytelling, and he too composed tender notebooks filled with cuttings and private palaces. Out of Schwitters's glowing documents, out of De Stijl but with Mondrian's compact pressures, Richard Meier emerges, with El Lissitzky his roommate.

Richard Meier signs and dates his collages as part of a lyrical autobiography, just as the best poems of certain poets, say Catullus or Frank O'Hara, are their collected poems. The works are damp with daylight and as sudden as Motherwell's famous *Lyric Suite*. In tearing his famous purity, in reassembling this as "torn architecture," Meier creates his own private museology of the mind. The ensemble flickers with all that Schapiro found in Picasso's *Chair Caning* of 1912: proper nouns and pronouns and lots of abstract notations, actions of a grown-up Situationist, who wearily turns down infantile *détournement* for a melancholy late poetics of Eros, still.

Architecture, Richard used to tell me, was his site of the purity, of the "hypothesis of perfection." I have also suggested architecture is the fragile, tragic, private, truth-telling art par excellence. Collage gives him a grand permission for imperfections that are stubborn words in Wallace Stevens's ode to hot dissonance.

These collages are a language, as much as Ashbery says he found in fabrics left in his childhood attic. Not for nothing are most of Meier's collages in other languages, except for a haunting doubled "Richard" as an addressee. This is Meier's Proun Room; each strophe is a contained room, and it adds up to architectural journeying, where no one can be interrupted.

Schwitters was making the degraded everyday meet the marvelous by negative capability. In Meier, all of these collages are sturdy as wall houses. The color red acts as intimately as any seduction, and his diagonals and drastic scrapes are all part of a learned style of opposition and meditation. Some of these papers, for example *Impruneta*, have the minimal exaltation of a Twombly. Different ochres are as eloquent as a moss garden—the "different mosses" in Pound's phrase. See *588* where a single calendar is turned into a very jazzy Stuart Davis in a most strident world. Here and elsewhere, Meier represents himself, his loves, his foreign ports, as language itself. It would be interesting to compare all this with Miró's obsessive postcards. But, finally, the architect, more than the painter, sides with the forces of gravity and makes up in a lover's quarrel with rectilinearity. Meier and his beloved white/black of Le Corbusier come back with torn edges of a very conscious architecture. Shelter is here temporary shelter and what Michal Govrin calls "the laws of temporariness."
These nudes, these haunted tickets, this foreign exchange and security checks—all of this is a strip search at night for a communal bricolage. Meier, like an astronaut, can save the rocket with a few cardboard pieces and a broken gadget or crayon.

I have often been seduced by the moment in *La Jeteé* where lovers from past and future come together in a Museum of Natural History, within whose bins and vitrines and upon whose walls hang the whole evolution of animals and lost animals. There, birds are described, but the image is still. Meier's series of collages are one cinema in which you may search for the opening of an eyelid. The scale is as adequate as Duchamp's valise and as portable as an oil painting made for a donkey's back. If the world exists to end in this book, perhaps it concludes in this critique of purity, these shattered bits, these uncertain memories, those we love, how we speak, what we mostly do not know, and the happy form of the questions we must pose.
Red and black, nudes like the news, Russian as photos on graves and Pasternak on snow, melting secretly from within, these are also temporary refuge.

New York, December 14, 2004

michael kurcher $\frac{1}{8}$
                                                                       $\frac{8}{87}$

743   /06AUG

ota

n:
elli
ork

Mod. 24   ESPRESSO
(EXPRÈS)

Lufthans

SECTION
X147
634
ADM. PRICE
AUG

ne28

GOOD ONLY
12:30 P. M.
BOX SE
ADMISSION $30.00
No Refunds - No Exchanges
1986

CENTER
DE Top, Damrosch Park)
For Circus Arts

ERG

HOLL
2301 N

26
5
93

30
9
87

bruxelles
russel
25.14.11

4

.53

RICHARD MEIER
136 EAST 67TH STREET
NEW YORK 10022
USA

l'agend

INSTITUT DE FRANCE
DOMAINE DE CHANTILLY
MUSÉE CONDÉ
Entrée pour 1 personne

N° 013049 | **20,00 F**

KET DOIT ÊTRE CONSERVÉ PAR LE VISITEUR

Richard Meier

indfahrt dem
MERSEE
nate Erholung!
NSCHIFFAHRT
Stegen (0 81 43) 2 29

Impruneta

York 10018

michael l-meier

11/7/90

DIENST DER GEMEENTEWERKEN

Postbus 19350

2500 CJ 's-Gravenhage

ION * Sábado 8 de setiembre de 1979 * Påg. 17

LA FUNDACION JOAN MIRO

0197

0197

Y GRAY

ART 1952

T VERLAG

18

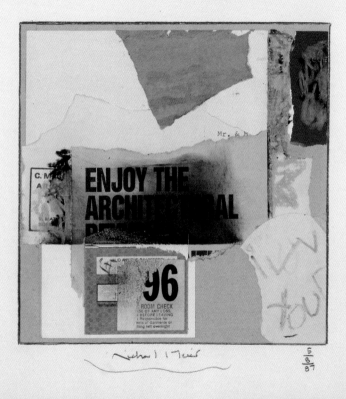

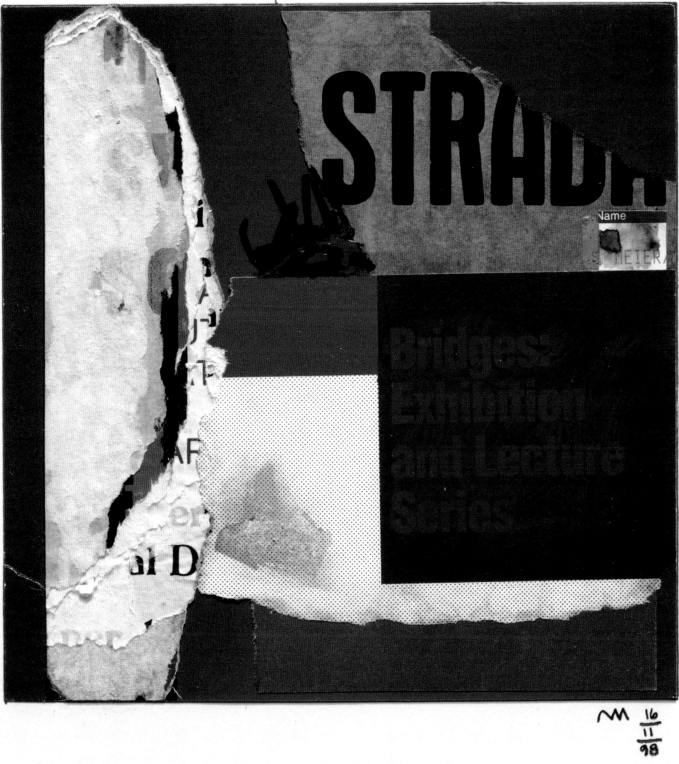

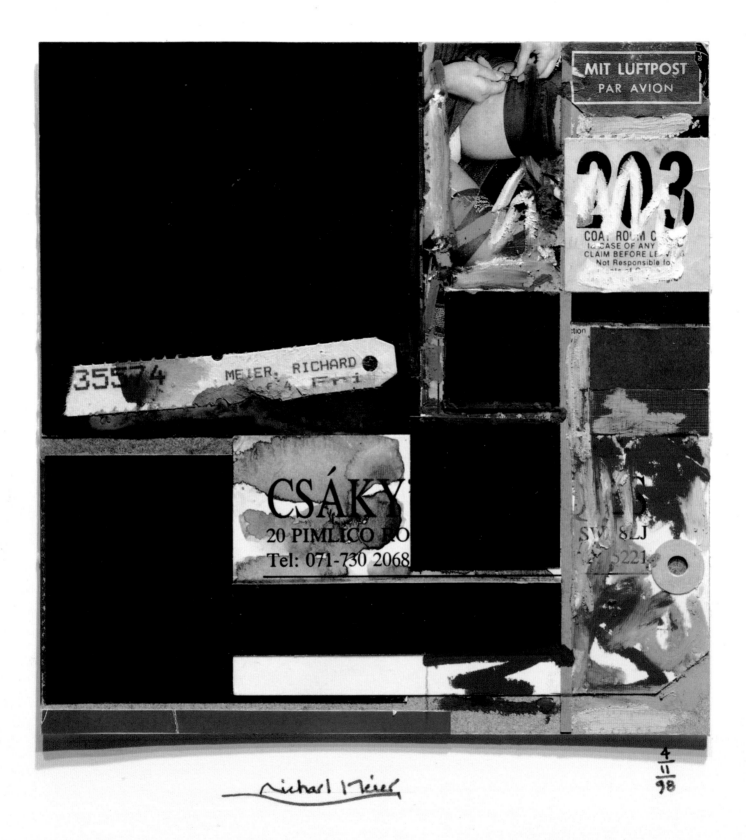

MIT LUFTPOST
PAR AVION

203

COAT ROOM C
In CASE OF ANY
CLAIM BEFORE LE
Not Responsible fo

35574   MEIER, RICHARD

CSÁKY
20 PIMLICO R
Tel: 071-730 2068

SW 8LJ
5221

Richard Meier

4
11
98

FOUNDED 1983, VOL. X, NO. 84, SEPTEMBER 1998 £4.50

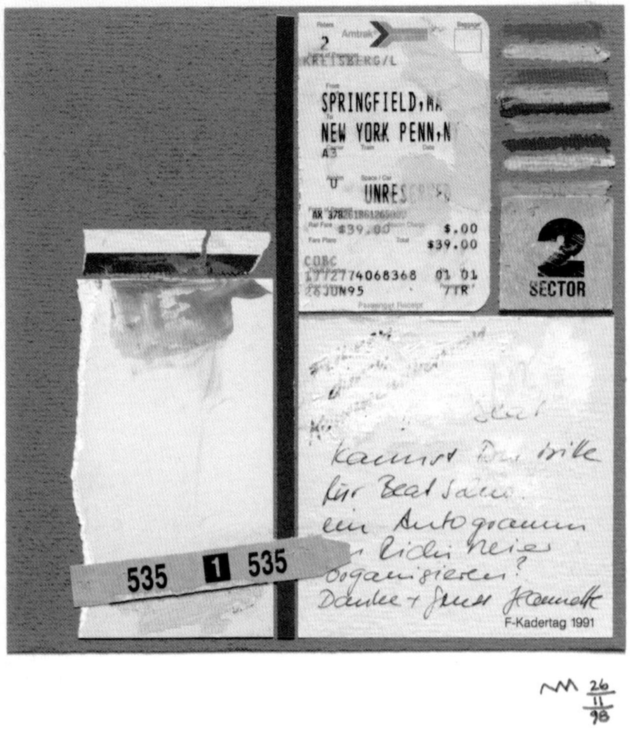
Amtrak
SPRINGFIELD,MA
NEW YORK PENN,N
$39.00
$.00
$39.00
26JUN95
2
SECTOR
535 1 535
F-Kadertag 1991
26/11/98

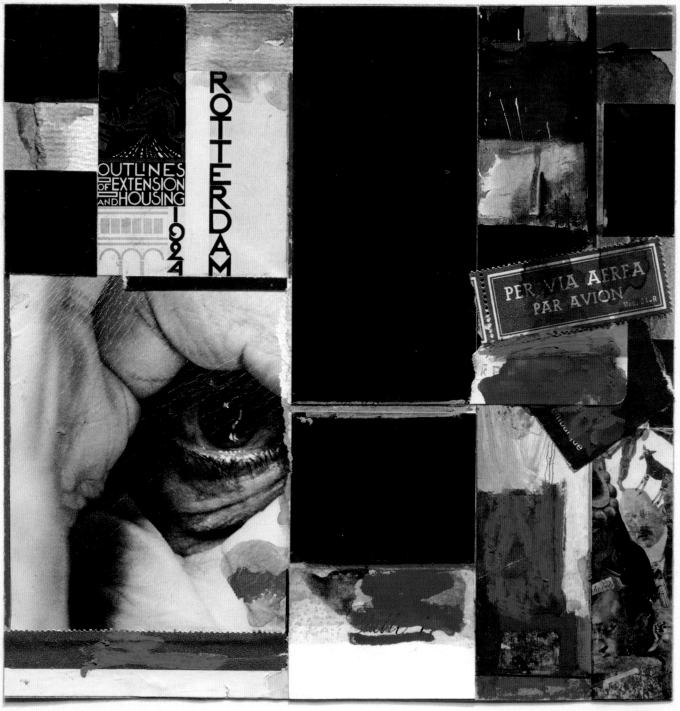

richard meier

Michael Meier

12
Apr
1999

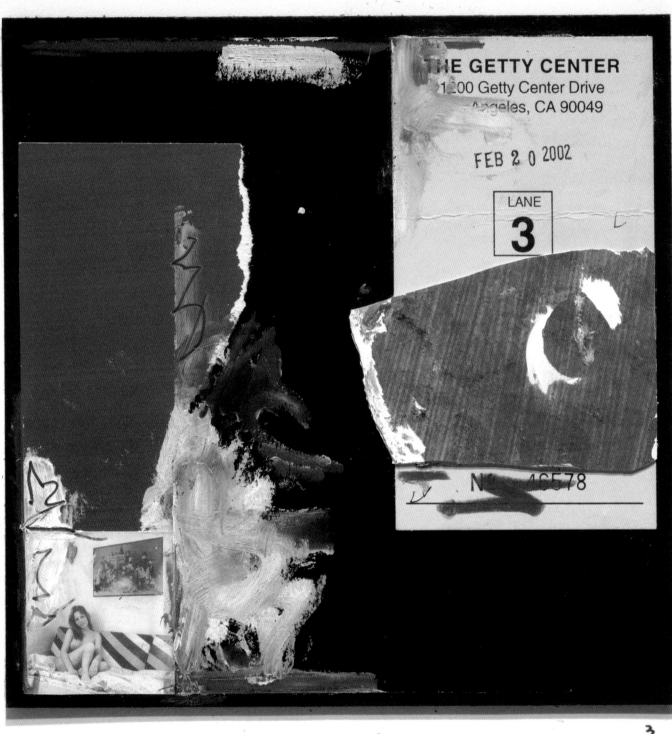

THE GETTY CENTER
1200 Getty Center Drive
Angeles, CA 90049

FEB 2 0 2002

LANE
3

NO 46578

Michael Meier

АНИЯ, СИЛЫ,

with the exhibit...

Michael Teien

16/8/87

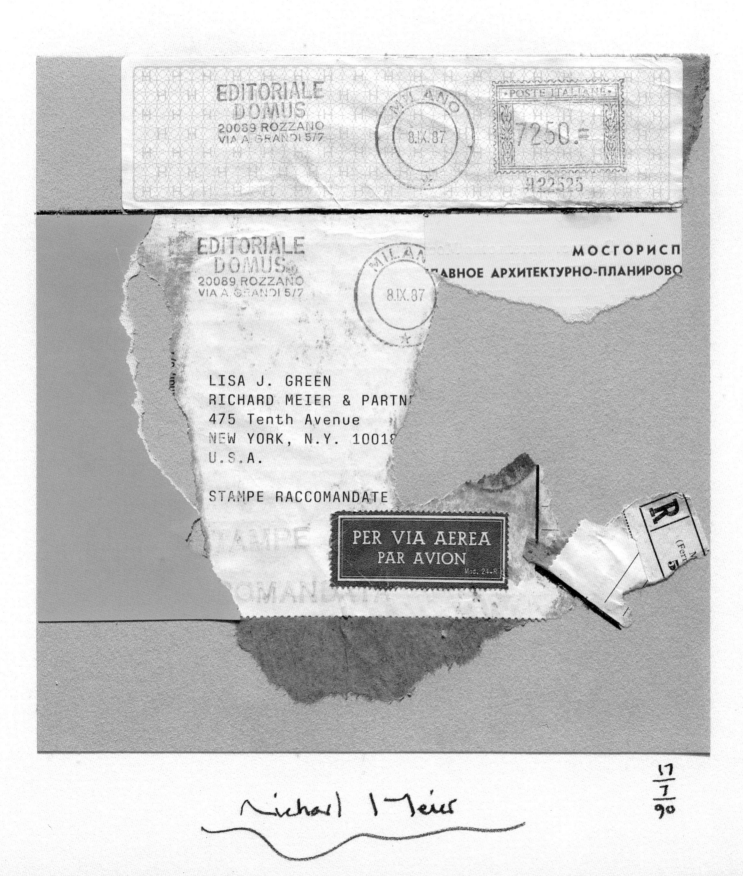

EDITORIALE
DOMUS
20089 ROZZANO
VIA A. GRANDI 5/7

MILANO
8.IX.87

POSTE ITALIANE
7250.=
422525

EDITORIALE
DOMUS
20089 ROZZANO
VIA A. GRANDI 5/7

MILANO
8.IX.87

МОСГОРИСП
ГЛАВНОЕ АРХИТЕКТУРНО-ПЛАНИРОВО

LISA J. GREEN
RICHARD MEIER & PARTNE
475 Tenth Avenue
NEW YORK, N.Y. 10018
U.S.A.

STAMPE RACCOMANDATE

PER VIA AEREA
PAR AVION
Mod. 24-R

R
M
(Ferr
5

ШЕНИЙ

Michael Meier

14/9/87